THE ANCIENT GREEKS
THEIR LIVES AND THEIR WORLD

ALEXANDRA VILLING

The J. Paul Getty Museum, Los Angeles

Published in 2010 in the United Kingdom by
British Museum Press
A division of The British Museum Company Ltd
Alexandra Villing has asserted her right to be
identified as the author of this work.
Designed and typeset by John Hawkins
Cover design by Jim Stanton
Printed in China at C&C Printing Co Ltd

Published in the United States of America in 2010 by
The J. Paul Getty Museum, Los Angeles

Getty Publications
1200 Getty Center Drive, Suite 500
Los Angeles, California 90049-1682
www.getty.edu/publications

Library of Congress Control Number: 2009939813

ISBN 978-0-89236-985-0

On the front cover: Head of a marble statue of Apollo
from Cyrene (North Africa), 2nd century AD, after
a Hellenistic original. Racing chariot on an
Athenian black-figure Panathenaic prize-amphora
of the late 5th century BC. Symposion scene on an
Athenian red-figure drinking cup painted by the
Kodros Painter, *c.* 430 BC.

Illustration Acknowledgements

Unless otherwise noted below, the photographs in this book
show objects from the collections of the British Museum.
They were taken by the Photographic and Imaging
Department of the British Museum and are
© The Trustees of the British Museum.

The map on page 6 was drawn by Cally Sutherland.

The colour reconstruction of the Parthenon metope on page
39 is a British Museum computer-generated photograph.

© age fotostock/SuperStock: 14 bottom left.

J. Paul Getty Museum, Los Angeles, wine jug with
knucklebone players, attributed to the Group of Boston,
10.190, Greek, Athens, about 420 BC: 28 top right.

The Royal Collection © 2009, Her Majesty Queen
Elizabeth II: 18 top right.

Alexandra Villing: 9 top, 24 top left, 38 left, 58 top, 73 top.

CONTENTS

Introduction 4

Map of Greece 6

Timeline 7

1 Kings and Tyrants 8

2 Democrats and Citizens 12

3 Gods and Goddesses 16

4 Heroes and Heroines 20

5 Priests and Priestesses 22

6 Families and Children 26

7 Craftsmen and Artists 34

8 Farmers 40

9 Slaves 44

10 Writers, Thinkers and Doctors 48

11 Entertainers 54

12 Athletes 60

13 Soldiers 66

14 Traders and Travellers 72

Find Out More 78

Index 79

INTRODUCTION

> There is the Greek people – our common blood and language, the sanctuaries and sacrifices to the gods that we share, and our common way of life.
>
> Herodotus

Who would you have been, if you had lived in ancient Greece? A seafaring trader? A famous wrestler or boxer? The wealthy ruler of a city-state? A slave working in the silver mines? A priest or priestess of a god? A fisherman or shepherd? A soldier in Alexander the Great's army? A professional dancing girl? A potter, gold-smith, or weaver? There were many different ways for people to live in ancient Greece. And much of what they did has influenced the way we live today.

An Athenian lady with her maid, a young slave girl.

Greece was not a big and powerful empire like ancient Rome. Instead, for most of the time the ancient Greeks lived in small independent city-states and kingdoms. Athens, Sparta, Thebes, Corinth – each city fiercely protected its own character and freedom. They often quarrelled with each other: for land, for natural resources, for power. But they also knew that they all shared the same language and gods, and sometimes – when faced with danger from outside – they all united to fight together.

A bronze figurine of a Greek warrior.

Ancient Greece (called 'Hellas' by the Greeks themselves) consisted of a mountainous mainland surrounded by the sea and hundreds of islands. So it is not surprising that the Greeks – like their mythical hero, Odysseus – were great seafarers and traders. They sailed all around the Mediterranean Sea, as far as Syria, Egypt, North Africa, Italy, France, Spain, and even Britain. In many places they founded cities of their own. The Greeks learned a lot from the foreigners they met and traded with, especially from the peoples of the ancient Near East and Egypt. But they also spread their own Greek art, stories and language across much of the ancient world.

Terracotta figures of two girls playing a game of knucklebones.

Whatever they did, ancient Greeks were always trying to outdo each other: in fighting, in theatre, in sport, in science or philosophy, in architecture and crafts. Perhaps this is one of the reasons why the Greeks achieved so much. Even today there is much in our daily lives that goes back to their ideas and culture. They were the first in Europe to use coins. Many of our words and the ideas behind them are of Greek origin: **air, athlete, barbarian, gigabyte, diet, history, school, philosophy, theatre, hero, tyrant**. We still celebrate the Olympic Games, 2700 years after they were invented. And even our form of government, democracy, is a Greek invention.

Look inside this book to meet the people behind those ideas, and find out about their lives and their world.

Marble statue of a Greek athlete, a discus thrower.

A Greek silver coin.

Map of Ancient Greece

TIMELINE

3200–1400 BC	The Minoan civilization on Crete and Thera.
1600–1100 BC	The Mycenaean civilization.
1184 BC	The end of the Trojan War, in Greek belief.
1000 BC	The Greeks settle the Aegean islands and the west coast of Turkey.
776 BC	First Olympic Games.
775 BC	Some Greeks begin to settle in southern Italy.
800–700 BC	The time of the poets Homer and Hesiod. The Greek alphabet is created.
700–480 BC	The Archaic period of Greece.
650–600 BC	Greeks begin to settle in Egypt, North Africa, the Black Sea area, France and Spain.
566 BC	The first Panathenaic festival at Athens.
561–510 BC	Peisistratos and his sons are tyrants at Athens. After them, democracy develops.
490–479 BC	The Persian Wars: the Persian Empire attacks Greece and is defeated.
480–323 BC	The Classical period of Greece. The time of the playwrights Aischylos, Sophokles, Euripides and Aristophanes, the historians Herodotos and Thucydides, the doctor Hippokrates.
462/1 BC	Radical democracy is established in Athens.
447–438 BC	The time of Perikles. The Parthenon is built on the Akropolis of Athens. Pheidias designs its sculptures.
431–404 BC	The Peloponnesian War between Athens and Sparta. Athens is defeated.
410–350 BC	The time of the philosopher Plato. The first philosophical school in Athens is founded.
399 BC	Trial and execution of the philosopher Sokrates.
350–300 BC	The time of the philosopher Aristotle and the politician Demosthenes.
336–323 BC	Alexander the Great conquers a huge empire.
323–31 BC	The Hellenistic period of Greece.
146 BC	The Roman army sacks Corinth. Macedonia and the rest of Greece are under Roman control.
31 BC	Battle of Actium. Augustus becomes the first Roman emperor, and Greece is part of the Roman empire.

1 KINGS AND TYRANTS

In the early days, around 2,700 years ago, Greece was divided into several kingdoms. This was the period we now call the 'Bronze Age', because bronze was the most common metal produced at that time. There were two great civilizations in this period, the Minoans on the island of Crete and the Mycenaeans on the Greek mainland.

EARLY KINGS OF GREECE

The first great Bronze Age civilization in Greece was that of the Minoans, who lived on the large and fertile island of Crete and on nearby Thera (Santorini). The Minoan rulers lived in big houses or palaces. The most famous was the palace of Knossos. Here the legendary King Minos was believed to have lived. According to later Greek stories he kept a wild and dangerous creature, the Minotaur, in a labyrinth at his palace. The Minotaur was part man and part bull, and demanded to be fed seven Athenian boys and seven girls every nine years. But the Athenian hero Theseus finally managed to kill the beast.

Theseus killing the Minotaur. A painting on an Athenian pottery jar.

Bronze figurine of a bull jumper. On Crete, somersaulting over the back of a bull was a daring sport for young people.

The famous Lion Gate of the city of Mycenae.

People on the Greek mainland were also ruled by kings who lived in large palaces. The main palace was at Mycenae. That is why we call these people the 'Mycenaeans'. The Mycenaeans were great warriors and eventually conquered the Minoans. Their cities had massive defensive walls built from huge rock boulders.

At the end of the Bronze Age, around 1100 BC, during a time of much upheaval, the palaces were destroyed and the system of kingdoms disappeared from Greece. Instead, from the eighth century BC onwards, most Greeks lived in independent city-states, or in the regions and villages that belonged to them.

LEGENDARY KINGS

Later Greeks had only a vague memory of this early part of their history, and they filled in the gaps with mythical stories of powerful kings and fabulously strong heroes, such as King Minos of Crete and the heroes Theseus and Herakles.

The Athenians believed that, once upon a time, their city had been founded by King Kekrops. He was half man, half serpent, and was said to have been born from the earth itself.

King Kekrops.

TYRANTS

At first, most Greek cities were ruled by a few wealthy aristocrats. Sometimes one of them became more powerful than the others and took control by force. Such rulers were called 'tyrants', but the word did not yet have the negative meaning it has today. Sometimes tyrants were cruel and bad, but sometimes they were good and everyone prospered. Under the long rule of the tyrant Peisistratos and his sons, Athens became wealthy and powerful and Athenian arts and crafts flourished.

> In general Peisistratos caused the people little trouble during his reign, but always encouraged peace and quiet. For this reason the tyranny of Peisistratos was often talked about as a golden age.
>
> Aristotle

This painting, on a drinking cup, may show the Athenian tyrant Peisistratos and one of his sons in a chariot, surrounded by warriors.

ALEXANDER THE GREAT

Alexander the Great was one of the greatest military leaders in the history of the world. He was king of Macedonia, in the north of Greece, which was one of the few areas that kept its kings. His father King Philip conquered many Greek cities and brought to an end the time of independent city-states. When Philip was killed in 336 BC, Alexander took the throne.

> He did not want to inherit a kingdom that offered him riches, luxuries and enjoyment, but he preferred struggles, wars and unrelenting ambition.
>
> Plutarch

Alexander set off immediately on new conquests. In 334 BC he and his 50,000 soldiers crossed the Hellespont – the narrow strait separating Europe and Asia.

Marble portrait of Alexander the Great.

A coin showing a warrior on horseback attacking a war elephant. This may be Alexander the Great, fighting with King Poros of Punjab.

Within four years Alexander defeated the Persian Empire and conquered Asia Minor, Egypt and Mesopotamia. However, after he had defeated King Poros of Punjab (on the border of modern India and Pakistan) his soldiers rebelled. They had grown tired of the long campaign. Soon after, in 323 BC, Alexander died of a fever in Babylon, aged 32. His huge empire was divided up into smaller kingdoms by his generals. His conquests had affected many peoples and cultures and spread Greek influence over a huge area – Alexander had changed the world of the ancient Greeks for ever.

Statue of King Ptolemy I (305–283 BC) as pharaoh of Egypt. Ptolemy I was one of Alexander the Great's Macedonian generals and he ruled Egypt after Alexander's death.

This is probably a portrait of the Egyptian queen Arsinoe II (278–270 BC). She was the daughter of Ptolemy I. In Greece itself, women could not be rulers, but Egypt had a long tradition of powerful queens. The last and most famous was Cleopatra.

2 DEMOCRATS AND CITIZENS

Democracy was invented by the ancient Greeks. 'Democracy' comes from the Greek word *demokratia*, which means 'the people's rule'. Athens was the first place in history where the people (in Greek, *demos*), whether rich or poor, ruled their city. Many other Greek cities also had democratic constitutions.

This relief may show a man voting in Athens. The man holds out his hand above a hydria, a water jar. Water jars were used as urns to collect votes in the Athenian Assembly.

It all started in Athens when the tyrant Hipparchos, son of Peisistratos, was murdered. After his death, a handful of wealthy and powerful Athenians competed for power. One of them, Kleisthenes, introduced changes that allowed ordinary people to take more part in politics.

Harmodios and Aristogeiton, the two men who killed the tyrant Hipparchos, became heroes for the Athenians. This painting shows the statues of the two 'tyrant slayers' that the Athenians set up in their market place.

You two will be famous forever,
Dearest Harmodios and Aristogeiton,
Because you killed the tyrant and made
Athens a city of equal rights.

Athenian drinking song

But the final push for 'people power' came when, in the early fifth century BC, Athens was attacked by the mighty Persian Empire. The city managed to fend off the attack only because all the people, rich and poor, fought together as one. In particular, the poorest Athenians, who rowed in the warships, were crucial in securing victory. Soon after, equal political rights were given to all Athenian citizens.

The sea captains, the time-beaters, the ship-masters, the look-out officers and the shipbuilders — they are the ones who give strength to the city, far more than the foot soldiers, the high-born, and the honourable citizens. It therefore seems right that everyone has a share in the public offices, elected or chosen by lottery, and that any citizen can speak his mind if he wants to.

The Old Oligarch

A bronze juror's ticket inscribed with the name of its owner, 'Aristophon, son of Aristodemos'. Every Athenian citizen had such a ticket. They used the tickets to take part in the decisions made by juries in law courts.

THE CITIZENS' ASSEMBLY

Every male citizen of Athens could take part in the Assembly, the Athenian parliament, which met every ten days. To ensure that even the poor could afford to take time off from their work, everyone who attended was paid by the city.

On Assembly day, at dawn, thousands streamed up the streets to the Pnyx, the hill where the Assembly met to discuss and vote on all sorts of matters of importance for the city. They must have been lively gatherings. People stepped on to the speaker's platform to make speeches. There was applause, protest, heckling or laughter from the crowd. Men who were particularly clever and spoke convincingly could become very powerful politicians. But there was also a special safeguard: if someone had become too powerful, the people could vote to send him into exile for ten years. This process was called 'ostracism'.

> Even those of us who are engaged in business have a very fair knowledge of politics ... and we regard someone who takes no part in public affairs as good for nothing.
>
> Speech by Perikles, quoted by Thucydides

PERIKLES

The most famous Athenian statesman was Perikles (495–429 BC). He was a powerful speaker in the assembly and for fifteen years in a row he was elected to be one of the military leaders of Athens. This is why his portraits show him wearing a general's helmet. During his time Athens was the richest and most powerful of all Greek city-states. It became the leader of a league of Greek cities. Perikles also convinced the Athenians to build new temples for their gods. The Parthenon, the most splendid temple of them all, still stands today on the Athenian Akropolis.

LAWS AND INSCRIPTIONS

The many laws and decrees passed by the Athenian people in the Assembly were all engraved in stone and publicly displayed. In this way everyone could check exactly what the law said.

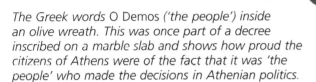

The Greek words O Demos *('the people') inside an olive wreath. This was once part of a decree inscribed on a marble slab and shows how proud the citizens of Athens were of the fact that it was 'the people' who made the decisions in Athenian politics.*

> It is true that we are called a democracy, because the administration is in the hands of the many and not of the few. In law, all men are regarded as equal in their private disputes, but reputation also counts. When a citizen has in any way distinguished himself, he is preferred for public office, not because of his connections, but because of his virtues. Poverty is not an obstacle for public service, as even the most ordinary man can do good things for the state.
>
> Speech by Perikles, quoted by Thucydides

Left: The Parthenon in Athens; a portrait of Perikles.

The Athenian Assembly passed many decrees honouring the good deeds that individual people had done for the city of Athens. Such decrees were often decorated with a relief showing Athena, the city goddess of Athens, crowning the honoured person.

NOT QUITE A PERFECT SYSTEM?

Ancient Greek democracy did not actually mean that everyone had a say. Of the 300–400,000 people who lived in Athens in the fifth century BC only 10 or 15 per cent were allowed to participate in politics. Why so few? Because only free male adults with an Athenian father could be citizens. Women, slaves and foreigners living in Athens could not take part at all.

3 GODS AND GODDESSES

The ancient Greeks believed in many different gods and goddesses. They imagined the gods as an extended family and told many stories about their adventures and especially their encounters with mortals. In these stories the gods seem very human. They can be happy or sad, friendly or nasty, winners or losers. But at the same time they are always immortal and powerful, and they had to be worshipped accordingly. The twelve Olympian gods were the most important, but there were also many lesser gods.

THE MAIN GREEK GODS

Zeus was the highest of the Greek gods and the head of the family of gods. He was a weather god, and he is often shown with a thunderbolt in his hand. The Olympic Games in Olympia were held in his honour. He was married to Hera, and was the father of many other gods and heroes.

The Greek god of shepherds and flocks was called Pan. He was part-man and part-goat. On this mirror-lid you can see him playing a game of knucklebones with the goddess Aphrodite. Pan was one of the many minor gods worshipped by the Greeks.

The gods at a feast: Poseidon and Amphitrite, and Zeus and Hera. Can you spot who is who, based on their dress and the objects they hold?

Zeus, holding a big thunderbolt, is giving birth to Athena – look how she pops out of his head, fully armed! Hephaistos is running off, scared.

Hera, the wife and sister of Zeus, was the queen of the Greek gods. She was the protectress of marriage, but her own marriage to Zeus was rather difficult. Zeus had many love affairs with other goddesses, and mortal women as well. Hera is often shown with a veil (the dress of brides and respectable women) and a royal sceptre.

Poseidon, a brother of Zeus, was the god of the sea, but also of earthquakes and horses. He was married to Amphitrite. His special attribute was the trident – a three-pronged fork for catching fish.

Athena was the goddess of war and wisdom and the main patron goddess of Athens. The story of her birth is a strange one. Her father Zeus had swallowed her pregnant mother, Metis, to avoid Athena being born. But Zeus soon got a terrible headache and asked the smith god, Hephaistos, to split his head open to ease the pain, and out popped Athena. Refusing to get married, she forever remained Zeus's special daughter. Her attributes are a shield, spear and helmet as well as a protective magical cape called the *aegis*.

Hephaistos, a son of Zeus and Hera, was the god of smiths and other craftsmen. When he was a baby, Hera threw him out because he had a crippled foot, but luckily he was rescued. He was a skilled craftsman and made Athena's special protective cloak, the *aegis*. He was married to the goddess Aphrodite.

Apollo sits in front of an altar holding a kithara and an offering bowl.

Apollo, son of Zeus and brother of Artemis, was the god of music, arts and healing. He is usually shown as a beautiful, long-haired young man. He often carries a lyre or a *kithara* (a musical instrument), and a bow and arrow, as he was also an expert archer. His sanctuary at Delphi was the most important oracle in the Greek world, and many people went there to ask the god for advice.

Artemis, goddess of the hunt, is attacking a deer.

Artemis was the twin sister of Apollo. She was a hunter (often shown carrying a bow and arrow) and a protectress of wild animals. She roamed the woods and remained a virgin forever, just like Athena. She was the patroness of young girls before marriage.

Demeter, a sister of Zeus, was the goddess of grain and farming. The Greeks believed that Demeter's daughter, Persephone, spent each winter in the Underworld (the world of the dead). While Persephone was away, Demeter was so sad that the plants stopped growing. This is how the ancient Greeks explained the cycle of the seasons.

Ares, a son of Zeus and Hera, was the god of war. The war goddess Athena was good at clever strategy and defence, but Ares was more aggressive and violent.

Aphrodite was the goddess of love and beauty, but also of politics and sea travel. Her companion was Eros, a young boy representing the idea of love. She was married to the lame smith god Hephaistos, but she had many other lovers.

Marble statue of Aphrodite bathing.

Hermes, a son of Zeus, was the messenger of the gods. He was the patron of travellers, but also of thieves. You can recognize him by his messenger's staff and his travelling hat and boots.

Dionysos, a son of Zeus, was the god of wine, dance and disorder, and the patron of the theatre. His companions are the satyrs, wild beings part-man, part-beast, who get drunk and misbehave, and Maenads, wild women who perform frenzied dances.

Dionysos, holding a drinking horn and a vine branch. Behind him stands the messenger god Hermes. The goddess carrying two children may be Aphrodite.

The Underworld. The old man seated on the left is Hades (also called Pluto), king of the Underworld. Persephone, holding sheafs of grain, is being led away by Hermes for her yearly return to the world of the living. To her right, Sisyphos is carrying a huge boulder – the gods condemned him to live for eternity in the Underworld and to push a big rock up a hill only for it to roll down again and again.

Hades, a brother of Zeus, was the god of the Underworld. The Greeks believed that, after they died people's souls went to live in the Underworld, which they imagined to be a rather sad and gloomy place.

STRANGE GODS

Every little detail and aspect of ancient Greek life was covered by the gods in some way or another. For example, at Olympia Zeus was worshipped as *Zeus Apomyios*, 'averter of flies' – people could pray for his help to make sure that flies would not annoy the athletes and spectators during the Olympic Games.

FOREIGN GODS

Greek religion was very flexible and tolerant. The Greeks did not mind at all if others believed in different gods. In fact, they often added foreign deities to the large family of Greek gods.

One such foreign goddess was Bendis. She was a hunting goddess worshipped in Thrace, north east of Greece. Her cult was introduced into Athens by immigrants from Thrace. Bendis reminded the Greeks of Artemis, and her cult soon became popular with the Greeks too.

Athenian marble relief showing Bendis receiving worshippers. How do we know this is Bendis? She wears a foreign, Thracian-style dress and an animal skin.

4 HEROES AND HEROINES

Heroes such as Herakles, Theseus or Achilles were the stars of Greek myths. They were mortals but had special powers. Some heroes were the children of a god and a mortal while others came from ancient royal families.

THESEUS

Theseus was a special hero of Athens. He was the son of the god Poseidon and a mortal mother. He killed many dangerous beasts who had been making people's lives a misery, and eventually became king of Athens.

This Athenian drinking cup shows some of Theseus' most famous deeds. In the centre, he has just killed the monstrous Minotaur of Crete and pulls him out of the labyrinth. Around the edge, Theseus is fighting with Skiron, a robber who fed people to a giant flesh-eating turtle; he faces the ferocious sow of Krommyon; he kills the bull of Marathon; he wrestles with Kerkyon; he kills the robber Siris by tying him between two pine trees and letting them snap apart; and he attacks the cruel bandit Prokrustes, who used to invite travellers to sleep on his bed. If they did not fit in, he either stretched them or chopped off their feet. Can you spot which deed is which?

HERAKLES

Herakles was the most famous of Greek heroes. He was the son of Zeus and a mortal woman, and he was enormously strong. Herakles' weapon was the club and he wore a lion skin cape. Herakles' most famous adventures were his 'twelve labours', or tasks:

1. Kill the Nemean Lion.
2. Kill the nine-headed Hydra.
3. Capture a wild boar and bring it to King Eurystheus. (The king was so scared, he hid in a storage jar.)
4. Get rid of the vicious Stymphalian birds.
5. Clean out the Augean stables.
6. Obtain a horn from the wild deer of Keryneia.
7. Capture the Cretan bull.
8. Tame a herd of man-eating horses.
9. Fight the Amazon queen and take her girdle.
10. Steal cattle from the monster Geryon.
11. Overcome Cerberus, the three-headed dog that guarded the Underworld.
12. Steal golden apples from the nymphs called the Hesperides.

HEROES OF THE TROJAN WAR

The most famous Greek myth is that of the Trojan War. The war began when a Trojan prince, Paris, ran away with Helen, Queen of Sparta. The Greek army besieged Troy for ten years, and in the end destroyed it. Experts still argue about how much of the story is true.

The main characters in the story are young warriors such as Achilles or Hector. But there are also heroic girls, such as Iphigeneia, the most widely worshipped of all Greek heroines. Her father, Agamemnon, was told to sacrifice his daughter to the gods in order to help the Greeks win the war. Heroically, Iphigeneia agreed to die. In some versions of the story, she was saved by the goddess Artemis.

Agamemnon stands at the altar and is about to sacrifice Iphigeneia, but the goddess Artemis saves her by putting a deer in her place. Look closely and you can see the deer appearing behind Iphigenia.

5 PRIESTS AND PRIESTESSES

Religion played a big part in everyone's life in ancient Greece. Worshipping the gods was important to ensure the welfare of every person but also to ensure the welfare of the state. Every god had a priest or priestess to look after the god's sanctuary and rites. This was an important official role which both women (usually in cults of female gods) and men (usually in cults of male gods) could hold. Priests and priestesses sometimes inherited their office and sometimes they were appointed, elected or – in democratic Athens – chosen by lot.

In most of Greece, being a priestess was the only major public role that women could have. One such priestess was Choirine. In the 4th century BC she was a priestess in the important cult of the grain goddess Demeter at Eleusis, near Athens. She is shown here on her gravestone holding the symbol of her office, the key to the temple door. Choirine's name means 'Piglet' – pigs were sacred to Demeter.

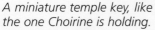

A miniature temple key, like the one Choirine is holding.

Priests and priestesses had to organize festivals, perform sacrifices and make sure that the rites were performed properly. There were many religious festivals in ancient Greece. They were occasions for large groups of people – whole villages, cities or regions, and sometimes even people from all over Greece – to come together. Festivals took place in the open air outside the temple. They could go on for several days and could include musical, theatrical and athletic competitions. The high point of most festivals was the sacrifice of animals, such as cattle, goats or sheep.

A portion of the meat was burned on the altar for the gods. Then the rest of the meat was roasted and eaten by the whole community.

On this bowl you can see a rural festival with a procession of men, including musicians. They are leading a bull to the altar, behind which Athena, goddess of war and wisdom, is standing. This may be a statue of the goddess or an imagined 'presence'. At the head of the procession is the priestess. She carries on her head the sacrificial basket containing grain and the sacrificial knife that will be used to slit the bull's throat.

On this pot we see what happens after the animal is killed. The meat from the slaughtered animal is being roasted on spits over the altar, on which the portions for the god are burning. The priest is pouring an offering of drink for the god.

For Athena Nike a priestess shall be chosen by lot from all Athenian women ... The priestess shall receive fifty drachmas as well as the thighs and skins from the communal sacrifices.

Athenian decree of 448 BC

SANCTUARIES

The most important places in Greek religion were the sanctuaries of the gods. They were often in a special natural setting. At the heart of the sanctuary were the altar,

The temple of Hephaistos at Athens.

where sacrifices to the gods were performed, and the temple, which housed the cult statue of the god.

People came to the sanctuary to pray and to leave gifts for the gods, which could be anything from large, expensive statues to small, cheap pieces of pottery or figurines. People gave these offerings to thank the gods and also to ask for their help in the future.

This wine jar shows a cult statue in a temple. The large three-legged bowls (tripods) beside the temple are probably gifts to the god.

One special gift for a god was a sacred garment for the god's statue. The most famous is the *peplos* robe, which was woven by a group of girls for the cult statue of Athena at Athens. Here you see a boy handing the finished *peplos* to an official.

This was the central ceremony of a special yearly festival. The scene was carved on a frieze that ran around the Parthenon temple at Athens.

When they reached the temple of Athena in the upper city, lovely Theano, daughter of Kisseus and wife of Antenor, opened the doors, for the Trojans had made her the priestess of Athena. The women lifted up their hands to Athena with sacred cries, and lovely Theano took the robe and placed it on Athena's knees, while she was praying to the daughter of great Zeus: 'Lady Athena, protectress of our city, mighty goddess, break the spear of Diomedes and let him fall before the Skaian gates. Do this, and we will sacrifice in your temple twelve cattle, if you will take pity on the town and wives and little children of the Trojans.' So she prayed, but Pallas Athena rejected her prayer.

Homer

THE TOMB OF A GREEK PRIESTESS

These objects – a gold necklace, ring and sceptre – were found together in the grave of a priestess. She is also shown holding the sceptre on the engraving on the ring. It was a symbol of the power she had on behalf of the deity, or god, she served. Who was this deity? Have a close look at the necklace.

Among the pendants are two female heads with horns. The horns tell us that this is Io. In Greek myth Io was a priestess of the goddess Hera. She was turned into a cow by Zeus and she is often shown as a woman with cow's horns. Therefore, archaeologists believe that the woman buried in the tomb must have been a priestess of Hera.

ORACLES

The most powerful priestess in Greece was the Pythia at Delphi. She delivered the oracles (advice) of the god Apollo. Delphi was the most important oracle in Greece and people consulted the Pythia on anything from politics to personal problems.

The Pythia sat on a tripod – a large bowl on three tall legs – over an opening in the earth from which the ancient Greeks believed intoxicating spirits rose. Her answers were often given in riddles, which the priests of the temple helped to interpret.

At another oracle at Dodona, the priestesses and priests had to interpret the rustling of leaves in the sacred trees, through which Zeus and Dione were believed to speak. Some of the questions people asked the gods at Dodona have been found by archaeologists:

Kleotas asks Zeus and Dione whether it would be better and profitable for him to keep sheep.

Herakleidas asks Zeus and Dione whether he will have children with Aigle, the wife he has now.

The god Apollo, holding a musical instrument, and his sister Artemis stand in front of the omphalos. The omphalos was a big stone at Delphi that was believed to be the navel of the world.

6 FAMILIES AND CHILDREN

For the ancient Greeks, the heart of everyone's life was the *oikos*, meaning 'the household'. The *oikos* included not just parents and children, but also grandparents and slaves, all living together.

THE GREEK HOUSEHOLD

The head of the household was the father. He and the older sons spent most of their time out and about, in the city, in the gymnasium, in the shop, in the fields, or even at war. Women, girls and young boys under the age of seven stayed at home.

A Greek household: a father and mother are saying goodbye to their son who is going off to war. A naked young boy – perhaps a brother or a slave – is carrying the liver of an animal that has just been sacrificed to the gods. If the liver was healthy this was a good omen. The young man behind the mother may be another brother or slave.

Greek houses were usually not very big. They were two storeys tall with an inner courtyard where most of the housework was done. Slaves and masters lived closely together. Women were responsible for all the housework, including wool-working and cooking. Greek women had far fewer rights than men.

As regards the relationship between male and female, the male is by nature superior and the female inferior.

Aristotle

For a woman it is more appropriate to stay at home than to go out; but for a man it is shameful to stay indoors rather than to occupy himself with business outside.

Xenophon

A mirror of the type used by Greek women. The bronze surface would originally have been silvered and polished to make it reflective.

This pot shows an Athenian housewife spinning wool, while a slave girl holds a perfume vessel and a sash.

Two women doing housework. These terracotta figurines show one woman sitting in front of an oven and another grinding grain.

BABIES

For babies born in ancient Greece, the first few days were a dangerous time. Often babies died very young. If there was something wrong with a baby, the parents were allowed to abandon it. To show that a baby was being accepted into the family, its father would carry it around the fireplace at the centre of the house. The baby was given a name when it was ten days old.

A baby-feeder, with the words: 'drink, don't drop!'

A child sitting on a potty and waving a rattle. A toy roller is propped up against the wall. On the floor you can see a miniature jug, just like the one on which this scene is painted.

A nurse hands a baby to its mother. In front of the mother's chair is her wool basket.

PETS AND TOYS

Just like children today, Greek children played games and had pets and toys. Here are some examples.

Greek boys playing knucklebones.

Three ancient Greek knucklebones. The ankle joint bones of sheep and goats were cheap and popular toys in Greece.

NURSES AND TUTORS

Most families had a nurse for any young babies, a female nanny for the girls and a male teacher for the boys. Even though these people were often slaves, they were much-loved members of the household.

Terracotta figurine of an old nurse with a baby.

A girl is teasing a dog by dangling a tortoise in front of it. She wears a short patterned tunic and amulets across her chest and round her ankles.

A doll with movable arms and legs, made from clay.

After children had grown up they often dedicated their toys to a god.

Philokles here hangs up these toys of his boyhood to Hermes: this perfect ball, this clattering boxwood rattle, the knucklebones with which he so often fiercely played, and his spinning top.
Leonidas

Timarete, before her wedding, has dedicated her tambourine, her pretty ball, the net that protected her hair, her dolls, and her girl's dresses to Artemis of the Lake, a girl's gift to a girl, as is proper.
Anonymous Greek poem

This is the tomb stone of Melitta, nurse of Hippostrate. Melitta is shown seated with little Hippostrate standing before her. The writing says:

Here the earth below covers the good nurse of Hippostrate: now she misses you. While you were alive I loved you, nurse, and now I honour you still, though you lie below the earth, and I will honour you as long as I live. And I know that even beneath the soil, if there is any reward for the good, you above all, nurse, have honours lying in store with Persephone and Pluto.

EDUCATION AND GROWING UP: BOYS

A good education is one that improves both the mind and the body.

Plato

A young boy having a riding lesson. He grabs the horse's mane and throws his leg over its back, but still nearly falls off!

In ancient Greece, from the age of seven, the sons of better-off people went to school. Poorer boys might learn a trade or work on the family farm. At school, boys learned to read and write and to play music, and did a lot of sports. This was important, as even at a young age boys could compete in the Olympic Games. Damiskos of Messene won the Olympic boys' foot race at the age of twelve.

A bronze figurine of a Spartan warrior.

At the age of eighteen, Athenian boys entered military service for two years. Spartan boys, however, started their military training at age seven and lived in communal military barracks until they were 30, learning to be brave and obedient soldiers.

The painting on this small Athenian jug shows two boys practising their reading and music. One is reading from a long, rolled-up scroll of papyrus (this is what books looked like in ancient Greece), while the other holds a lyre.

If you were not at the exercise ground before sunrise, you would get quite a punishment from the gymnasium master! …. There you used to get your exercise, by running, wrestling, throwing the spear and discus, boxing, 'ball games and jumping'.

Then, when you had returned home from the horse-race track and exercise ground, you would sit neatly dressed on your chair before your teacher with your book, and while you were reading, if you missed a single syllable, your skin would be made as spotted as a nurse's cloak.

Plautus

EDUCATION AND GROWING UP: GIRLS

In Sparta, girls went to school alongside boys and also received an athletic education. In other Greek cities, girls were taught at home by their mother and nurse. They learned to spin wool, to weave cloth, to cook and to look after the household. Some girls also learned to read and write, which was useful if they ran a large household after they married.

Some girls also spent time as cult servants in temples. Each year a few girls, called *arrephoroi*, were chosen to spend time in Athena's sanctuary on the Athenian Akropolis. It was a great honour for the girls.

> Once I was seven I became an *arrephoros*. Then at ten I became a grain-grinder for the goddess. After that, wearing a saffron robe, I was a yellow 'bear' at Brauron. And, as a lovely young girl, I once served as a basket bearer, wearing a string of figs.
>
> A girl, speaking in a play by Aristophanes

Terracotta figure of a seated girl with a folded writing tablet open on her knee.

Marble statue of a little girl with her pet birds. Such statues were set up for girls who had been cult servants in the sanctuary of Artemis at Brauron; they were called the 'bears of Artemis'.

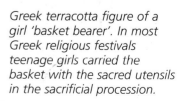

Greek terracotta figure of a girl 'basket bearer'. In most Greek religious festivals teenage girls carried the basket with the sacred utensils in the sacrificial procession.

BRIDE AND GROOM

A marriage procession as painted on an Athenian vase: the groom is taking the bride on a chariot to his house, the door of which is just being opened by a maid. Friends and family members follow, carrying blazing torches and gifts.

> They were leading the brides from their homes by torchlight through the city, and loud rose the bridal song; young men were spinning about in dance, and there was the sound of pipes and lyres, and women stood in their doorways and admired it all.
>
> Homer

Girls got married very young in ancient Greece, from the age of about 13. The husband would be much older, about 30 years old. Marriages were usually not love matches, but a way to create links between families and to produce children to continue the family line.

Ancient Greek weddings lasted for several days. On the first day the bride took a bath in sacred water and offered her old clothes and toys to the goddess Artemis. On the second day there was a big feast and, in the evening, a large procession to take the bride from her parents' home to her new husband's house. On the next day friends and relatives dropped in with gifts.

> I put a spell on the rite and marriage of Thetima and Dionysophon ... May he take no woman but me.
>
> A Greek love-curse

If the marriage did not work out, divorce was relatively easy in ancient Greece – a husband could simply send his wife back to her family! Women, too, could ask for a divorce, with the help of a male relative. The most common reasons for divorce were the wife's unfaithfulness or the failure of the marriage to produce children. Not being able to have children was seen as a curse from the gods.

> If a husband and wife get divorced, she shall have her own property that she came with to her husband, and half of any income from her own property, and half of whatever she has woven, and five staters [coins], if her husband is the cause of the separation; but if the husband denies that he was the cause, the judge shall decide.
>
> Law of the city of Gortyn on Crete

DEATH AND BURIAL

For the Greeks it was natural to honour their parents, and their other ancestors, after death. Funerals were important occasions. The body was laid out on a special stand called a bier and a coin placed in the mouth for the mythical ferryman, Charon, who took the dead person's soul across the river Styx into the Underworld. Before sunrise, the body was taken from the house to the cemetery outside the city walls by a procession of relatives, pipe players and, sometimes, professional mourners.

Relatives placed gifts into the grave, such as pottery, jewellery or toys. A large vase, a statue or a tombstone stood on top of the grave. Relatives would visit the tomb regularly on the birthday of the dead person and on particular festival days; they would pray and sing mourning songs and leave more gifts for the dead.

An Athenian oil flask. Such flasks were often brought to the grave as a gift, and were decorated with appropriate scenes. On this flask you can see a woman visiting a grave with a tall gravestone. On its steps stand a flask and other vessels. The woman holds another oil bottle.

A Greek funeral: a procession of mourning men and women moves towards the bier, on which the body of a young man lies, his head propped up by a cushion.

7 CRAFTSMEN AND ARTISTS

Metalworkers and carpenters, smiths, potters and painters, sculptors and architects – these and other skilled craftsmen were the people who created all the objects and buildings that we admire today from ancient Greece.

Craftsmen's workshops once clustered around the marketplaces of Greek towns. A few crafts that were particularly dirty and dangerous, such as potters' workshops with their firing kilns, were on the outskirts of town. Workshops were often sociable places. The Greek writer Hesiod warned farmers not to waste their time hanging around the smithy, and we know that the philosopher Sokrates used to gather his young students in the workshop of Simon the shoemaker near the Athenian marketplace.

Perfume bottles in the shape of two sandalled feet.

This picture of a shoemaker is painted on the inside of a drinking cup. If you look closely you can see that he is working on a sheet of leather, which he will eventually turn into a boot or shoe, just like the ones hanging on the wall behind him.

Craftsmen did not have a very high social status in ancient Greece. Many were also not proper citizens, but resident foreigners with limited rights, or even slaves. Still, it is obvious that they took great pride in their work.

> You will see for yourselves, here are all kinds of shoes ... slippers ... boots ... Argive sandals ... flats ... Say what is the heart's desire of each one of you!
>
> Herondas, a shoemaker

AN UNHAPPY METALWORKER

> Lesis is sending a letter to Xenokles and his mother. Do not forget that he is perishing in the metal workshop but come to his masters and find something better for him! I have been handed over to a thoroughly wicked man; I am dying from being whipped; I am tied up; I am treated like dirt more and more!
>
> Letter written on a piece of lead by the Athenian apprentice boy Lesis

In a smithy, a seated craftsman is heating a piece of metal in the blazing fire of a furnace. He and his colleague are shown naked, appropriate for the hot and sweaty conditions in a smithy.

CRAFTSWOMEN

There were also female craftworkers in ancient Greece. Women did not usually work in metal and pottery workshops. They could be fullers (somebody who cleans newly woven cloth), cobblers, or confectioners, or they could make and sell shoes, perfume, wreaths, ribbons, bread, sweets or porridge. But most often they were woolworkers and made and sold wool, cloth and clothing.

A woman is spinning in this drawing on an Athenian jug. She is holding a ball of wool high on a stick from which she twists a fine thread with the help of a rotating spindle at the bottom.

A spindle, spindle whorls and a miniature wool basket.

Wealthier women generally stayed at home, supervising the work of slaves and spinning wool and weaving cloth, together with all the female members of the household. The cloth was for the family's own use and sometimes also for sale.

THE POTTER'S CRAFT

Greek potters created some of the most beautiful and elaborate pots ever made. Over many centuries they worked out a perfect technique to produce fine, but sturdy, pots with a flawless finish. Fine Greek pottery, particularly from Athens, was sold to many places outside Greece.

Greek potters made all sorts of pots, from large storage bins and amphorae to little perfume vessels and drinking cups. The pots were shaped on a potter's wheel and then designs were painted with a fine 'slip' – this was a finer, runner version of the same clay from which the vase was made.

A potter is making a drinking cup on his potter's wheel. Some finished cups are already stacked up on a shelf behind him.

A firing gone wrong! This stack of small dishes has melted together because the kiln became too hot.

Greek potters had a special secret – they fired their pots for hours and hours in a very hot pottery kiln. This was the crucial stage. Many things could go wrong and all the potters' work could be spoiled in one careless moment. The potters prayed to the gods – particularly Athena and Hephaistos, the patrons of craftsmen – for divine help. But if all went well, the pots came out dry and hard. The painted parts of the surface had turned a shiny, glossy black and the rest of the pot a deep orange, showing off the patterns and scenes that had been painted on to them so skilfully. These images on pots usually depict myths or scenes of daily life – like many of the examples you see in this book – and they tell us much about the lives of the ancient Greeks.

An Athenian drinking cup painted with a pair of eyes.

If you pay me for my song, O potters,
Then come, Athena, and hold your hand above the kiln!
May the cups and all the bowls turn a good black,
May they be well fired and fetch the right price,
Many being sold in the marketplace and on the street,
And bring in much money, and may my song be pleasing.
But if you turn shameless and dishonest,
Then I call the kiln destroyers,
Smasher and Crasher and Reduce-to-ashes and Shake-to-pieces
And Terminator of the Unbaked, who makes much trouble for this craft:
May they stamp on stoking tunnel and chambers, and the whole kiln
Turn into a mess, while the potters cry and scream.

Greek poem

An Athenian wine jar (amphora) decorated with the mythical fight between the hero Achilles and the queen of the Amazons, Penthesilea. It was potted and painted by Exekias, one of the best Athenian vase painters.

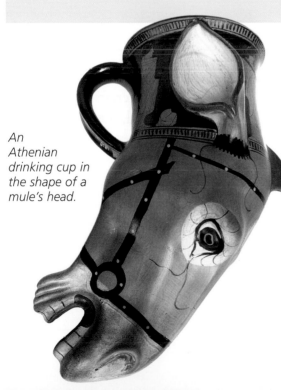

An Athenian drinking cup in the shape of a mule's head.

FAME AND FORTUNE

In later periods some craftsmen – especially painters and sculptors – became famous and their works commanded high prices. The painter Apelles of Kos, for example, was said to have been paid 20 gold talents (this is an enormous sum – about 500 kg of gold) for a portrait of Alexander the Great. The Greeks praised artists particularly for their ability to paint realistic scenes. One story tells how an artist painted some grapes so lifelike that birds tried to peck at them.

ARCHITECTS

Greek architects and engineers were masters of their art. They designed some of the most amazing buildings of the ancient world: huge temples, city walls, towers, tunnels, lighthouses, water clocks, catapults, water supply systems, and much more. Some details of Greek architecture are so subtle that they are hard to reproduce even with modern technology.

The temple of Poseidon at Sounion, near Athens.

SCULPTORS

Pheidias was one of the greatest sculptors of Classical Greece. His huge cult statue of Zeus at Olympia was one of the Seven Wonders of the Ancient World. At Athens he designed the marble sculptures that decorated the Parthenon, the large temple on the Akropolis. They are considered the high point of Classical Greek art. Look at how the horses rear up, with their manes flying, and the riders' cloaks fluttering.

Horsemen from the Parthenon frieze.

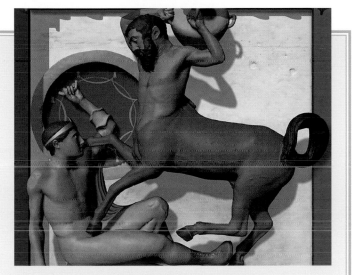

This is a sculpture from the Parthenon as it would have originally looked. Greek sculptures and temples were, in fact, very colourful, but the paint and the metal details have disappeared over the centuries.

JEWELLERS

Greek craftsmen produced wonderful pieces of jewellery: necklaces, finger-rings, armlets and earrings. Gold was particularly popular and was shaped into flowers, leaves or berries, such as myrtle buds, ivy leaves or acorns, but also into animals and mythical creatures.

These are some of the earliest Greek earrings known. They are only about 3 cm in diameter, but have elaborate patterns made of tiny balls of gold (as small as 0.2 mm in diameter), which the jeweller stuck to the gold surface. Producing this incredibly fine work must have been very difficult and hard on the eyes.

A gold necklace with seed-like pendants and green and blue enamel decoration. The wide chain from which the pendants hang was 'knitted' out of a thin gold wire about 30 m long.

8 FARMERS

For ancient Greeks, life was dominated by the agricultural year. Many Greeks were farmers and lived on small family farms in the countryside or in villages. They grew the grain (especially barley) that was the staple of the ancient Greek diet. Barley was used to make porridge and bread.

Farmers had a hard life, because of the threat of pests and droughts, and also because of the frequent wars. Armies swept across the land and destroyed crops, farms and villages. Farmers prayed to the grain goddess, Demeter, for divine protection against all these troubles.

To Pan of the goats and fruitful Dionysus and Demeter Lady of Earth I dedicate a common offering, and beg from them good flocks of sheep and good wine and good grain to be gathered in the harvest.

Anonymous Greek poem

When the Pleiades (stars) ... rise, begin your harvest, and your ploughing when they set ... Sow naked and plough naked and harvest naked, if you wish to bring in all Demeter's fruits in due season.

Hesiod

On this Athenian cup, a farmer is ploughing while a boy sows.

Marble statue of the goddess Demeter.

Ploughing and sowing were normal everyday activities, but the picture on the pot on page 40 may actually show a special ploughing connected with a festival of Demeter.

Why do we think this? Look at the other side of the cup, at the top of this page. A group of dancing women is moving towards an altar. This must be a religious festival. The woman standing behind the altar is holding a special type of basket that was used for separating the grain seeds from the chaff (winnowing). So we know that she is a priestess of the grain goddess Demeter. Farmers made sacrifices to Demeter to thank her for good harvests.

We are on our way to a harvest festival. Friends of mine are holding it for divine Demeter. They are presenting her the first-fruits of their wealth, because the goddess has piled up plenty of barley on their threshing floor!

Theocritus

The Greek diet was rich and varied. As well as grain, farmers grew many types of vegetable and fruit, grapes for wine, and olives. Olives, from which olive oil was made, were especially important. They were under the protection of the goddess Athena – the deity of war, but also of crafts and civilization.

Of course, farmers also had animals. The Greeks kept geese and hens for eggs, and herds of sheep and goats whose milk they used for cheese. These herds were looked after by shepherds roaming the mountainous regions of Greece. This bronze figurine is a shepherd. You can just spot the ram's head popping out from underneath his cloak.

Farmers beat the olive trees with sticks to make the ripe olives fall. Boys also climbed up into the trees to shake the branches.

A hunter returns with his catch.

Greeks loved to serve fish on painted platters like this one, decorated with pictures of fish and seafood. (Can you see the little squid?)

Animals were too valuable to slaughter regularly for food. The ancient Greeks ate meat only rarely, most often at festivals or when hunters had managed to catch wild birds, hares or even boars. For those close to the sea, there was also fish. Many Greeks prized fish above all other foods.

LONGING FOR THE COUNTRYSIDE?

To live in the country on a small farm, far from the business of the market place, owning your very own pair of oxen, to hear the bleating of your sheep and the sound of the newly-pressed wine trickling into the vat, to snack on little wild birds, and not to wait around for small fish from the market that is three days old, overpriced, and has been weighed by a crooked fishmonger ...

Aristophanes

You might think that everyone in Greece really appreciated farmers, shepherds and fishermen. But even though city-dwellers envied country people for their plentiful resources, they also often looked down on them for being smelly, ignorant and stupid.

9 SLAVES

For the ancient Greeks it was entirely normal to own slaves. Perhaps about a quarter of the men, women and children who lived in ancient Greece were slaves. They could be anything from house servants to mine-workers. In Classical Athens alone there were as many as 100,000 slaves.

An Athenian lady hands her cloak to her maid. Unlike the mistress, the maid has short hair. This shows that she is a slave.

A Persian slave girl in Athens? The girl holding her mistress's jewellery box wears patterned trousers, a tunic and a cap. These are not Greek clothes, but the typical dress of some Near Eastern peoples.

GREEK VIEWS ON SLAVERY

> It is clear, then, that some men are by nature free, and others by nature slaves, and that for the latter the condition of slavery is beneficial and just.
>
> Aristotle

> God gave all men their freedom, and nobody was made a slave by nature.
>
> Alkidamas

Slaves were the property of their masters and they had few freedoms or rights. In some parts of Greece, such as in Sparta, whole populations of rural regions were slaves or servants of the dominant city. Almost every Greek, except for the very poor, owned at least one or two slaves. Buying an unskilled slave would have cost about as much as buying a new family car today, a skilled slave perhaps double that. There were large central markets for slaves, such as on the Greek island of Delos. In the second century BC thousands of slaves could be sold there in a single day.

FROM RAGS TO RICHES?

Sometimes slaves were set free by their masters, or managed to save enough money to buy their freedom. This is what happened to Phormion, a foreign slave in fourth-century BC Athens. He inherited his master's bank and shield factory, married his widow and became a respectable Athenian citizen. But Phormion was lucky. Life was nothing like that for most slaves in ancient Greece.

WHO WERE THE SLAVES?

Where did the slaves come from? Many of the slaves in Greece were foreigners from regions north of Greece, from Asia Minor, Africa and other places. There was a feeling among Greeks that most foreigners were naturally inferior to themselves. Often, foreign slaves were captured in war or kidnapped by pirates. But also Greeks themselves sometimes fell into slavery through war and piracy.

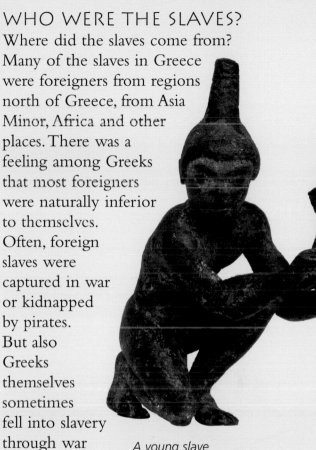

A young slave polishing a boot.

> About the same time that summer the Athenians besieged the city of Skione and forced it to surrender. They killed all the adult men and enslaved the women and children.
>
> Thucydides, describing what happened to the Greek city of Skione during the Peloponnesian War

LIFE AS A SLAVE

Many slaves worked on farms, helping in the fields and looking after animals. In the cities, slaves worked as nannies, maidservants, teachers, cooks, textile workers or in workshops. If they lived in the master's house they were often considered part of the family. Young slave girls collected water from the fountain, older women and men looked after children, and young boys served at drinking parties, carried their master's exercise gear to the gym, or went with him to war as shield-bearers or messengers.

This woman baring her breast to feed a baby is a slave working as a nurse. If you look closely you can see that her upper arm is covered in dots and angled patterns – such tattoos are typical of Thracians. Thracian women were particularly sought after as nurses in Greece.

I've just come from the fountain at dawn with my water jar. I had such trouble filling it, in the crowd and clash and clatter of pots, being pushed and shoved by slave-girls and tattooed servants!

Aristophanes

A water jar showing women at a fountain house.

An African boy carrying his master's scraper and oil bottle (for washing after exercise).

With her [my wife] was an elderly woman who had been my nurse, a loyal and trustworthy woman who had been set free by my father. She then lived with her husband ... but after his death, when she was old and had no one to look after her, she came back to me. I could not let my old nurse live in misery ... and my wife wanted me to leave such a woman in the house with her.

Pseudo-Demosthenes

Many slaves also lived on their own and worked in workshops or factories. Often they were skilled craftsmen. Such slaves worked alongside free men on big public projects, such as the building of the Parthenon, where free men and slaves were paid the same amount.

This special wine-amphora has a double wall to keep the wine cool. It was painted in Athens by a slave called Lydos, 'the Lydian', a foreigner from a region in modern Turkey.

Generally, slaves were treated well. As 'human tools' they were valuable, and the Greek philospher Aristotle remarked that only a fool would damage his own property. There were laws in Greece about the treatment of slaves, but masters were allowed to do things that we would think very cruel today. Whipping was common and it was even legal for slaves to be tortured if they were questioned by a court of law. Not surprisingly, slaves sometimes tried to run away.

Slaves owned by the state worked as policemen, clerks, and even public executioners. Many thousands of slaves worked in the silver mines and ore-processing factories of Attica, where they had very hard lives.

The most famous Greek runaway slave was Drimakos, from the island of Chios. He was a kind of ancient Robin Hood, and commanded a band of runaway slaves who lived in the woods. After his death he was worshipped as the 'gentle hero', as he had encouraged honesty among slaves and good treatment among masters.

Terracotta figurine of a runaway slave sitting on an altar. Altars and sanctuaries were places of refuge for runaways. This particular slave is a character from an ancient Greek comedy, played by an actor wearing a mask. Masks usually had large open mouths through which the actors could speak their lines.

10 WRITERS, THINKERS AND DOCTORS

The ancient Greeks valued knowledge and wisdom. Some of the earliest important thinkers, writers and doctors came from ancient Greece and their achievements are still held in high regard today.

PHILOSOPHERS

The word *philosophia* is Greek and means 'love of wisdom'. Philosophers in Greece were thinkers, scientists, astronomers, geographers, biologists, zoologists and theologians all rolled into one. They tried to understand the way the world works – both the natural world and the people living in it.

Great Greek philosophers, such as Plato or Aristotle, made observations about life and people that still make a lot of sense today.

A marble statue of the philosopher Sokrates. He was supposedly quite ugly – pug-nosed and fleshy-lipped – proving that beautiful thoughts don't require a beautiful body!

The Greeks sometimes found their philosophers annoying – especially when they criticized people's behaviour. But they also greatly admired them as teachers. Philosophers educated young men (not women) in philosophy, astronomy, zoology, botany, logic and rhetoric. In 388 BC Plato founded the first philosophical school – the Academy. It was attached to a gymnasium, so young men exercised their bodies and their brains.

SOKRATES

Sokrates (469–399 BC) is one of the most famous Greek philosophers. He spent much time talking to ordinary Athenians, questioning their views and values and trying to make them understand how to lead a good life. His conversations were recorded in writing by his pupils Plato and Xenophon. The Athenians eventually accused him of corrupting their youth and of not worshipping the gods properly, and he was sentenced to death in 399 BC.

Part of a broken Roman oil lamp showing Diogenes coming out of his tub.

WISE WORDS BY GREEK PHILOSOPHERS

Know yourself.

Inscription in the sanctuary of Apollo at Delphi

Through sickness we appreciate the value of health, through hunger that of satisfaction, through effort that of rest.

Herakleitos

When I see sea-captains, doctors, and philosophers, man seems to me the wisest of all animals; but when I see interpreters of dreams, and fortune-tellers and those who listen to them, and men puffed up with fame or fortune, then it seems to me that there is no more foolish animal than man.

Diogenes

DIOGENES

Diogenes was one of the most original characters among Greek philosophers. He lived in a large storage jar rather than a house. Here you see him emerging from his tub. Diogenes made fun of his fellow Athenians, criticizing them for being foolish and corrupt and too dependent on the luxuries of civilization. For example, he is said to have walked through the streets of Athens carrying a lamp in the daytime, claiming to be looking for an honest man.

WRITERS AND POETS

In this book, Herodotus of Halikarnassos sets out the results of his studies into history. He wants to preserve the memory of the past, and to record the great and amazing deeds of the Greeks and of foreign peoples, and in particular the reasons why they ended up at war with one another.

Herodotus

The ancient Greeks were the first historians. In the fifth century BC, Herodotus and Thucydides wrote down the events of the two great wars of their times, the Persian War and the Peloponnesian War, trying to understand why they had happened. Their books are our most important sources for Greek history.

Other Greeks wrote poems and plays for the theatre – both sad ones (tragedies) and funny ones (comedies). Homer (if he really existed, which some scholars doubt) was the earliest poet, and his long epic poems tell the dramatic events of the great Trojan War. Sappho was the most famous poetess and wrote many beautiful love poems. Aischylos, Sophokles and Euripides were considered the best writers of tragedies, and Aristophanes the funniest writer of comedies.

Some say a crowd of riders, others of soldiers, and others of ships, is the most beautiful thing on the black earth. But I say it is whatever a person loves!

From a poem by Sappho

A marble portrait of Sappho.

Homer

THE GREEK ALPHABET

In the eighth century BC the Greeks adopted the alphabet from the Phoenicians. Over time this developed into the alphabet we use today. Ancient Greeks wrote on scrolls made from leaves of the Egyptian papyrus plant, or scratched letters into wooden tablets covered with wax.

A seated young woman writing on a wax tablet. The scene is engraved on a gem stone.

A Greek inscription cut into a marble block. It reads 'Basileus Alexandros anetheken ton naon Athenaiei Poliadi', which means, 'King Alexander dedicated the temple to Athena Polias'. Perhaps you can almost read this yourself? ('King Alexander' is Alexander the Great.)

Ancient Greek		Modern alphabet
α	Alpha	a
β	Beta	b
γ	Gamma	g
δ	Delta	d
ε	Epsilon	e
ζ	Zeta	z
η	Eta	e
θ	Theta	th
ι	Iota	i
κ	Kappa	k
λ	Lambda	l
μ	Mu	m
ν	Nu	n
ξ	Xi	x
ο	Omicron	o
π	Pi	p
ρ	Rho	r
σ	Sigma	s
τ	Tau	t
υ	Upsilon	y
φ	Phi	ph (f)
χ	Chi	ch
ψ	Psi	ps
ω	Omega	o

DOCTORS

There was no proper training or university course to become a doctor in ancient Greece. Greek doctors learned from observation and from each other. They tried to cure diseases mainly by diet and lifestyle, but they also prescribed drugs, set broken bones, treated wounds and performed operations.

> For old ulcers on the fore part of the legs that become bloody and black. Pound the flower of sweet clover, mix it with honey, and use as a plaster.
>
> Hippokrates

Some Greeks had a low opinion of doctors:

> Having cut, burned, and tortured the sick in every imaginable awful way, doctors then complain that their fee does not match their good work!
>
> Herakleitos of Ephesos

This is the gravestone of the Athenian doctor Jason. He is shown examining a sick boy.

HIPPOKRATES

Hippokrates was the most famous of all Greek doctors. He believed that it was not the gods who randomly made people sick – rather, there were reasons for illnesses, such as infection. He and his followers wrote many books about the diseases they studied and the cures they prescribed. They also wrote down rules for doctors to follow. The 'Hippocratic oath' is still sworn by many doctors today.

> I will prescribe treatments for the good of my patients according to my ability and my judgment and never do harm to anyone ... Whatever I see or hear through my work and daily dealings with people which should not be spread around, I will keep secret and will never reveal.
>
> Hippocratic oath

Hippokrates on a coin of the island of Kos.

DIVINE HELP

Often Greek people turned to the god Asklepios to safeguard them against illness. There are many stories of miraculous healings by this god.

Patients who had been cured by the gods often left a small model of the cured body part in the sanctuary as an offering of thanks. This marble relief was offered to Asklepios by Tyche, apparently for healing her bad leg.

A statue of Asklepios.

Hermodikos of Lampsakos was paralysed. When he slept in the temple the god [Asklepios] healed him and ordered him to bring to the temple as large a stone as he could. The man brought the stone which now stands before the temple.

Inscription from the sanctuary of Asklepios at Epidauros

11 ENTERTAINERS

Music, dance and theatre were everywhere in ancient Greece. Young men and women danced and sang at home, at work and at religious festivals. Actors staged elaborate tragedies and comedies during festivals for Dionysos, the god of wine and song, and other gods.

There was poetry, song or dance for almost every occasion. Women sang traditional work songs while preparing food, and men sang while rowing the warships or drinking at a party. There were sad songs at funerals and happy songs at childbirth. Mythical events of the past were recited wherever people gathered. Poets became famous for lyrics that were on everyone's lips, and professional musicians and dancers were hired for parties. Music was played to accompany soldiers marching to war and athletes exercising.

Look closely at the man on the pedestal. He is competing in a poetry competition. As with a speech bubble in a modern comic strip, he has words coming out of his mouth: 'Once upon a time in Tiryns…'. This must be the first line of a poem he is reciting.

MUSICIANS AND SINGERS

> The well educated man should be able to sing and dance well.
>
> Plato

Musical education was a part of most boys' and girls' lives. Pupils were expected to do well, not least since many religious festivals featured competitions in musical performance and dancing. There were also contests for reciting stories, especially the long poems of Homer that tell the events of the Trojan War. Music was considered to be very powerful and good for people. The god Apollo was the divine patron of music and poetry.

In this painting on a small Athenian jug you can see a boy practising the barbiton. He is accompanied by his two pets – a dog and a bird.

A music lesson. A bearded teacher plays the barbiton, a type of lyre, and his young pupil plays the double-pipes. Can you see his puffed cheeks? The double-pipes were said to have been invented by the goddess Athena, but when she looked in the mirror and saw her ugly, puffed-up face while playing, she threw them away in horror!

A kithara player is stepping on to the podium in a musical competition. He clearly is expecting to win, as winged female figures, symbols of victory, are surrounding him. The judge of the contest sits on a chair on the right. The kithara was an elaborate version of the lyre with a wooden soundbox, and was played by professional musicians.

PARTY ENTERTAINERS

Come to dinner quickly, and bring your jug and a boxful of food! It's the Priest of Dionysos that sends for you. Hurry up, you're holding up the dinner! Everything else is ready: couches, tables, cushions, rugs, garlands, perfume, nibbles ... wheat puddings, cheese cakes, sesame-cakes, pasta-cakes and — oh yes, and lovely dancing-girls ... Come on, hurry!

Aristophanes

Greek men liked to hold drinking parties with their friends. These were called *symposia*. At such parties, the participants lay on couches and ate nibbles and drank wine mixed with water. They had witty conversations, told stories, sang and recited poetry, and played games. Women were not invited, except as entertainers – professional pipe players, dancers or acrobats.

A female acrobat.

Two young girls receive a dancing lesson. They are probably training to become professional dancers to perform at private parties.

MUSICAL INSTRUMENTS

We have very little idea of how Greek music actually sounded. But some ancient musical instruments have survived.

A scene of music-making painted on an Athenian amphora. Terpsichore sits in the centre playing a harp; Mousaios holds a lyre and Melousa the double pipes (auloi); a type of kithara *is hung up on the wall behind them. Mousaios was a mythical Athenian musician and Terpsichore one of the nine Muses – mythical patronesses of arts and music. In fact, the word 'music' comes from the Greek* mousike, *meaning 'the art of the Muses'.*

Men are relaxing on couches at a symposion.
They are listening to a girl playing the double pipes.
Look at the man next to the girl. His head is thrown
back and his mouth is open, which means that he is
singing a song.

Wooden
auloi (double
pipes) from Athens. They
were always played as a pair, and were one of
the most popular musical instruments of ancient
Greece. They look like flutes, but are actually more
similar to a modern oboe, and sound much stronger and
harsher. Some Greeks complained that they sounded
awful, like a screeching woman.

Left: A wooden lyre using a tortoise shell as a
soundbox. In myth, the god Hermes invented the
lyre, using as strings the intestines of a slaughtered
cow from the god Apollo's sacred herd.

As you sip your wine let these delicacies be brought
to you: pig's stomach and boiled sow's womb in
cumin, vinegar and silphion sauce, together with
tender roasted birds, of whichever species is in
season ... All other delicacies are a sign of hopeless
poverty — I mean boiled chickpeas, beans, apples,
and dried figs. But have a cheese cake from Athens,
and if you can only get one from somewhere else,
demand some Attic honey, as that will go with your
cake really well!
                                                        Archestratos

Symposia were meant to be civilized gatherings —
but sometimes the drinking got a bit out of hand:

The first bowl is to health, the second to love and
pleasure, the third to sleep. When this is drunk,
wise men go home ... The fourth bowl is to
violence, the fifth to shouting, the sixth to drunken
rudeness, the seventh to black eyes, the eighth to
getting into trouble with the law ...
                                                        Euboulos

The rowdy end to a symposion!

THEATRE AND ACTORS

At the festival of Dionysos, the Athenians, after having had their lunch and wine, went to the theatre. Wearing wreaths, they watched the plays, and drinks and snacks were served to them throughout.

Philochorus

Going to the theatre was an important event in ancient Greece. Plays were staged as part of big annual festivals for Dionysos, the god of the theatre, song and dance, and for other gods. At Athens every year, playwrights wrote sets of three tragedies and a satyr-play, as well as comedies, for the festival of Dionysos, and a jury decided which plays were best.

The plays were mostly spoken but also included music and singing.

The ancient Greek theatre at Epidauros. Greek theatres were usually semi-circular structures built against natural slopes of hills. The word 'theatre' comes from the ancient Greek word theatron, *which means 'the seeing place'.*

The audience (probably made up of men, women, children and slaves) would sit on stone benches in the open-air theatre and watch the performances – a marathon session of up to ten hours a day over three to four days.

Plays by the most famous Greek playwrights – tragedies by Aischylos, Sophokles and Euripides and comedies by Aristophanes – are still performed today.

The actors in this comedy wear particularly ugly, grotesque costumes and masks. You can see that the action is taking place on a wooden stage.

An actor playing the part of a young woman, wearing a female mask. Only men could be actors and so they also played female roles.

TRAGEDY AND COMEDY

Greek plays were often based on mythical stories, such as the great Trojan War. Tragedies tell stories of human suffering and could move everyone to tears, but comedies poked fun at everything and everyone – greedy politicians, nosy nurses, and bumbling heroes. Satyr-plays, too, were funny; they featured actors dressed as satyrs, part-man part-animal companions of the god Dionysos, who were always up to mischief.

Greek actors wore masks that showed what character they played. This is a terracotta mask of an African slave from a comedy.

A terracotta mask of an old man from a comedy.

The painting on this Athenian vase is based on a scene from Euripides' satyr-play Cyclops, in which the hero Odysseus and his companions blind the one-eyed monster Cyclops with a large stick.

Portrait of Euripides.

12 ATHLETES

Sport was central in the life of the ancient Greeks. Greek boys spent much of their time exercising in open-air gyms. Some would go on to compete in big all-Greek sporting festivals, such as the Olympic Games, founded in 776 BC. Large numbers of athletes and thousands of spectators from all over the Greek world flocked to Olympia for the games. There were also big sporting competitions at Delphi, Isthmia, Nemea and Athens, and many smaller local and regional ones. The games were usually held as a part of religious festivals.

The Olympic Games were loved and admired by the whole world, and here the Greeks showed their wealth, their strength, and their training. Not only were the athletes objects of envy, but also the victors' home towns became famous.

Isokrates

Four pentathletes: a jumper holding jumping weights, a discus thrower and two javelin throwers.

Major sports competitions allowed the Greek city-states to compete with each other in a peaceful way. Sport kept people fit, but it also encouraged discipline and endurance, which were useful in war and other civic duties.

People send their sons to a trainer ... so that they are not forced by the weakness of their bodies to behave like cowards in wars and in other duties.

Plato

Slaves and foreigners were barred from the Greek games. Girls and women did not regularly take part in sport – except in the city of Sparta.

[The Spartan lawgiver] Lykourgos believed that motherhood was the most important function of freeborn women. He insisted on physical training for the female no less than the male, and he introduced races and competitions of strength for women, since he believed that if both parents are strong they produce healthier children.

Xenophon

A scale model reconstruction of Olympia as it would have looked around 100 BC. You can see the temple of Zeus and other sanctuary buildings in the centre and the race course (stadium) at the far right.

A bronze figure of a Spartan girl running.

In most places, women were not allowed even to watch the games, though some managed to cheat the system by dressing up as men. A woman called Kallipateira managed to sneak into the Olympic Games dressed as a trainer to watch her son, Peisidoros, who was competing in the events. But when Peisidoros won, in the excitement of the moment she jumped over a fence and her cloak slipped off, and so she was found out.

GREEK SPORTS

Many different types of sport were practised in Greece – including foot races, wrestling, boxing, chariot- and horse-races, discus, javelin and jumping – and, strange to us, most of these were done naked. The ancient Greeks had different explanations for this custom. Some believed that the athlete Orsippos in 720 BC discovered 'that a naked man can run faster than one in a loincloth'. Others said that nudity was introduced because a runner once died after tripping over his loincloth.

BOXING AND PANKRATION

Boxing and pankration were the two events for fighters. Greek boxers wore leather thongs on their hands, not boxing gloves. The pankration was particularly brutal. It was a type of all-in wrestling in which almost anything was allowed. One famous pankratiast, Sostratos, was nick-named Mr Finger-Tips because of his trick of breaking his opponents' fingers. Another was Milo of Kroton, who between 536 and 516 BC won six Olympic titles in wrestling. He was a legendary figure who must have looked something like a modern day sumo-wrestler. He was said to prepare for fights by eating 8 kg each of meat and bread and drinking 10 litres of wine every day, and to train by running while carrying a cow on his shoulders!

Look closely and you can see that one of the boxers on this amphora has just been hit. Red blood is streaming from his nose.

Just as you, stranger, see the courage in this bronze image of Kleitomachos, so Greece saw his strength. For as soon as he had untied the blood-stained boxing thongs from his hands, he entered the fierce pankration. In the third event he did not dirty his shoulders with dust but, wrestling without a fall, won three contests in the Isthmian Games. He was the only Greek to win this honour, and Thebes of the Seven Gates and his father Hermokrates also won crowns.

Alkaios

In the scene on this drinking cup, a trainer is about to hit two pankratiasts who are trying to poke out each other's eyes. Eye-gouging was one of the few things that was actually forbidden even in pankration.

SOME EVENTS OF THE ANCIENT OLYMPICS

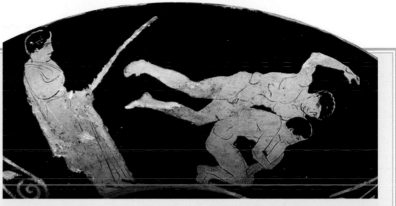

Wrestling

Javelin

Jumping

Foot races

Race-in-armour

Chariot races

Horse races

PRIZES AND HONOURS

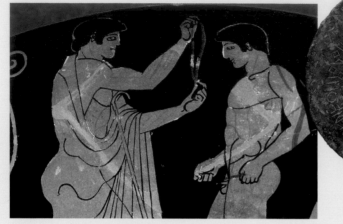

A winner being crowned.

Athletes often gave an offering of thanks to the gods for their victory. The inscription on this discus tells us that it is the very one with which Exoidas won the discus-throwing contest in Kephallenia, and that Exoidas dedicated it to Kastor and Polydeukes, the twin sons of Zeus.

Strong and fast athletes with muscular bodies were much admired by all and could win large prizes in sporting competitions. In the early fourth century BC, for example, the prize for winning the short sprint at Athens was sixty large amphorae full of best Athenian olive oil, worth nearly half the price of a house. At Olympia, however, winners only received olive branches and no money. Winners were always showered with honours and privileges by their home cities. Famous poets wrote poems about them and sculptors made statues of victorious athletes. One example is the bronze statue of a discus thrower by the sculptor Myron. The original statue is lost, but several marble copies made in Roman times still survive.

And all those who have won an athletic event at the Olympic, Pythian, Isthmian or Nemean Games shall have the right to eat free of charge in the city hall and also have other honours in addition to the free meals.

Athenian decree

Winners at the Olympic games even had a special ointment to cure pain and swellings. It was known as the 'victor's dark ointment'. It contained special ingredients, including opium. Today, the powerful painkiller morphine is extracted from opium.

Myron's statue of a discus-thrower.

CHEATING AND CRASHING

Like today, the prospect of great fame and wealth meant that athletes were tempted to cheat. The earliest known cheat at the Olympic Games was the Thessalian boxer Eupolos, who in 388 BC bought off three opponents to ensure his own victory. He and those he had bribed had to pay a big fine, and from this money six bronze statues of the god Zeus were erected on the road to the stadium, inscribed with messages warning others not to cheat.

The Olympic Games took place in honour of the god Zeus. A famous cult statue of Zeus, by the sculptor Pheidias, stood in the temple at Olympia. It looked similar to this small bronze figurine.

In fact, crashes happened in chariot races even when the racers were not cheating:

> They drew up their chariots ... At the sound of the bronze trumpet they shouted to their horses and shook their reins, and the whole course was filled with the clatter of rattling chariots ... But then the Italian's hard-mouthed horses went out of control and, in the turn of the sixth lap, crashed their heads into the car from Libya. As a result of this one mistake, cars kept smashing and colliding with each other, and the whole race-course was filled with broken chariots like a shipwreck.
>
> Sophokles

There are even Greek myths about cheating. One tells how Pelops bribed a charioteer called Myrtilos to 'fix' a race at Olympia. King Oinomaos had never been beaten in the chariot race, because he owned magical winged horses. Myrtilos tampered with the king's chariot, it crashed, and Pelops won the race.

A racing chariot.

13 SOLDIERS

War was common in ancient Greece. There were frequent disagreements between the many small city-states and also many larger wars – both within Greece and against foreign enemies, such as the Persians.

> It is a noble thing for a brave man to die in the front line, fighting for his homeland ... so let us fight with spirit for our land, die for our sons, and not spare our lives. Young men, fight shoulder to shoulder, do not start panic or shameful flight ... Let every man bite on his lip and stand, feet set apart, firm against the enemy.
>
> Tyrtaios

THE HEROES

In early times, the most famous battles were the duels between aristocratic heroes, such as Achilles and Hector. These warriors showed off their courage and fighting skills, wearing elaborate breastplates and helmets and wielding spears, swords and battle-axes. Many such fights are described in the poems by Homer, which record the events of the Trojan War, the most famous (but mostly mythical) war of the 'heroic' age.

Achilles, on the left, is darting forward with his spear towards Hector, who is wounded in the chest and thigh and is starting to collapse. In Homer's description, both heroes are wearing strong protective armour, but the painter of this pot shows them naked except for a helmet, shield, spear and a sword in a scabbard. This shows off the heroes' athletic bodies and makes their wounds look more dramatic.

As he [Hector] spoke he drew the sharp sword that hung so great and strong by his side, and gathering himself together he sprang on Achilles like a soaring eagle which swoops down from the clouds on to some lamb or timid hare ... Achilles, mad with rage, rushed towards him, with his awesome shield before his breast ... He looked Hector's fair flesh over and over to see where he could best wound him, but all was protected by the solid bronze armour — except at the throat, where the collar-bones divide the neck from the shoulders, a most deadly place. Here did Achilles strike Hector as he was coming towards him, and the point of his spear went right through the fleshy part of the neck.

Homer

THE *PHALANX*

After the collapse of the great kingdoms of the heroic age, a new battle tactic was developed. Citizens grouped together in a *phalanx*. This was a Greek invention, in which a group of armed soldiers marched and fought in a rectangular formation. Covering each other with their shields, they formed an almost impenetrable block while they attacked the enemy with long spears.

A typical Greek bronze helmet.

In this painting on a small perfume pot, a phalanx of warriors is locked in battle with the enemy. If you look closely you will see that the soldiers wear helmets like the one on this page.

GREEK SOLDIERS

All over Greece, young men were trained to be skilled and courageous warriors, but Spartan soldiers had the highest reputation of all. Spartan boys left home at age seven to live in barracks. They endured a gruelling training regime and were taught to be fearless and loyal, and that failure was not an option. It was said that one Spartan mother, Damatria, murdered her own son after he behaved like a coward in battle.

In Athens, male citizens at the age of eighteen swore an oath of allegiance to the city and entered a two-year military service. They spent one year on guard duty at the port of Athens, and the second year on garrison duty in a border fort. Some wealthy men became knights in the cavalry. Most Athenians, however, were armed foot soldiers (*hoplites*) fighting as part of the phalanx, or they rowed in a warship.

Here we see a soldier saying goodbye to his family and setting off to war. He is equipped with the typical soldier's gear – a large, round shield, a crested helmet, a metal breastplate with leather straps attached to its lower edge, a thin tunic underneath, greaves (armour for the shins), a sword in a scabbard and a spear.

A hoplite's equipment: a bronze breastplate, helmet and greaves (shin-guards).

> I will not bring shame on these sacred weapons nor will I desert the man at my side, wherever I am positioned in the line. I will defend what is sacred and holy. I will not pass on to my descendants my homeland smaller than I received it, but rather greater and stronger, as far as I am able to with the help of others.
>
> Athenian soldier's oath

An archer wearing Scythian dress. The Scythians lived on the northern Black Sea coast and were famous archers.

In addition to heavy infantry, there were also archers, 'slingers' and *peltasts*, who used javelins (throwing spears) and a *pelta*, a light wicker shield.

MERCENARIES

Well trained and well equipped, Greek soldiers were much in demand abroad. Greek mercenaries served in Babylon and Egypt, and in 401 BC a huge contingent of 10,000 Greek soldiers was hired by the Persian king Cyrus the Younger to help him seize the throne from his brother.

You have come home from the ends of the earth, with a gold and ivory handled sword …
fighting alongside the Babylonians you performed great deeds,
and you rescued them from difficulties
by killing a giant warrior nearly five cubits tall!

Poem by Alkaios, welcoming home his brother, who fought as a mercenary for the Babylonian king Nebuchadnezzar

A bronze figure of a Greek warrior on horseback.

A Phoenician silver bowl showing Greek mercenary soldiers attack a fortified city in the Near East.

FIGHTING AT SEA

Soldiers had to buy their own equipment, so most poor people – as well as foreign immigrants and slaves – participated in war as rowers in warships. The most advanced of these were the triremes. On these, 200 rowers sat in three tiers, each with his own oar, oarstrap and cushion, in very cramped and uncomfortable conditions. The Greek navy was crucial in the Persian Wars, when, against all odds, the Greeks with just over 300 (mostly Athenian) ships, defeated the 1,000-strong Persian fleet in the sea battle of Salamis in 480 BC. This battle preserved Greek freedom, and it also raised poor people's status and so paved the way to full democracy in Athens, where rich and poor citizens had equal say.

It was a Greek ship that began the attack ... At first the Persian fleet held its own; but when the mass of ships was crowded into the narrows ... each crashed its bronze-faced beak into another of their own line, and all of their oars shattered. The Greek ships, seeing their chance, hemmed them in and battered them on every side.

Aischylos on the battle of Salamis

The predecessor of the trireme was the bireme, with two tiers of oars. The bireme (on the right) has a prow in the form of a boar's head; four men have got up to furl the sails, while at the back the steersman sits with steering-oars and the landing-ladder. The bireme is about to ram a large merchant ship, so this is probably a pirate attack rather than a naval battle.

NEW TECHNIQUES OF WAR

During the many wars of the Classical and Hellenistic periods, new battle and siege tactics and technologies were developed. These included siege-towers, rams, catapults and the use of war elephants. If we can believe the story of the people of Megara, some were very inventive!

A coin from Carthage showing a war elephant.

During the siege of Megara, Antigonos brought his war-elephants into the attack. The Megarians, however, covered some pigs with pitch, set fire to them, and let them loose among the elephants. The pigs grunted and shrieked under the torture of the fire, and jumped forwards among the elephants, who were driven mad by this and all ran off in different directions. From this time onwards, Antigonos ordered the Indians to bring up pigs among the elephants when they trained them, so that the elephants got used to the sight of pigs and to their noise.

Polyainos

Warriors try to scale the walls of a city with a ladder and ropes.

14 TRADERS AND TRAVELLERS

The Greek philosopher Plato once said that the Greeks had settled on the shores of the Mediterranean Sea like 'frogs around a pond'. For the ancient Greeks, the sea was their element. Travel and transport by land was slow and cumbersome. Sailing was much easier and faster.

The Greeks were great seafarers and they knew how to build large, fast ships, and so the whole Mediterranean was their home. In search of fortune or treasure, but also fleeing from war or famine, the Greeks sailed and settled as far as Italy, Spain, North Africa, Egypt, Syria, Turkey and the Black Sea, and some even got as far north as Britain and Scandinavia.

A MYTHICAL TRAVELLER

In Greek legend, cunning Odysseus was the most famous Greek seafarer. After the Trojan War, the gods condemned Odysseus to sail the seas for ten long years before he was finally allowed to find his way home. During his travels he met many odd creatures in many strange lands. Among the most dangerous were the Sirens, creatures who were part bird, part woman, and whose irresistible songs lured sailors to shipwreck and death.

On this Athenian vase, Odysseus is just passing the island of the Sirens. He has made sure that his crew are wearing earplugs, and he himself is tied to the mast. In this way, they are all immune to the alluring song, but Odysseus can hear and enjoy it.

Overland transport was slow and cumbersome. Mules and donkeys were the main form of transport.

A typical Greek landscape – hills with olive trees, islands and the sea.

TRADERS

The Greeks bought and sold many goods across the Mediterranean, from staples, such as grain, oil, or copper ore, to luxury items, such as amber beads, rare spices or special wine.

From Cyrene there is silphion and cowhides;
from the Hellespont mackerel and all kinds of salted fish;
from Thessaly emmer-meal and sides of beef ...
Syracuse supplying us with pigs and cheese. ...
From Egypt come ships and papyrus;
and from Syria comes frankincense.
Beautiful Crete sends cypress wood for the gods,
while Libya has vast amounts of ivory for sale,
and Rhodes offers raisins and dried figs for sweet dreams.
From Euboea he brings pears and fat apples,
slaves from Phrygia, and mercenaries from Arcadia.
Pagasai supplies us with slaves and people with tattoos,
and chestnuts and shining almonds
are provided by the Paphlagonians,
as they are the ornaments of a feast.
Phoenicia, again, offers dates and wheat flour,
Carthage blankets and embroidered pillows.

Hermippos, on goods imported into Classical Athens

TRADE AND MONEY

Early on, traders paid for their goods in kind (by swapping one lot of items for another), or they paid with valuable items, such as precious metals or metal objects. And, of course, they paid with money – once coinage had been invented!

Traders used large pottery jars called amphorae to carry wine, oil, and also other goods, such as salted fish, almonds, figs and other foodstuffs. Greek amphorae have been found all over the Mediterranean area. Up to 3,000 amphorae fitted on a ship. In some ancient cities, archaeologists have found as many as 300,000 amphorae. So we know that there was a lot of trade going on in ancient Greece.

On this painting on a drinking cup, a youth lifts a large transport amphora. Around him, four large ships are sailing on the waves, accompanied by dolphins.

GREEK COINS

Coins were not known in Greece until about 650–600 BC. Some of the earliest examples were found in a small pot discovered underneath the temple of Artemis in the Greek city of Ephesos in Ionia (modern Turkey).

Ionians and the people of the neighbouring kingdom of Lydia are believed to have invented coins. These early coins were made of electrum – a mix of gold and silver and a little copper that occurs naturally in the Lydian river of Paktolos. Later coins were made of silver, bronze, and sometimes also gold.

This Athenian coin shows the head of the Athenian city goddess, Athena, and Athena's sacred animal, the owl. It has been cut open to check whether it is really silver all the way through. Ancient traders had to be careful. There were fake coins around that were made of copper and only coated with a thin layer of silver.

This is a trade amphora from Athens. Olive oil from Athens and wine from certain Greek islands were very popular all over the Greek world.

Some amphorae had stamps on their handles that functioned a bit like a label on a wine bottle. This one has a grape symbol next to the name Diodotos. So the amphora probably contained wine from Diodotos' estate.

Hermes was the divine patron of travellers and traders, but also of tricksters and thieves. He usually wears the big hat that all Greek travellers wore, but his winged boots were special to him alone.

Soon most cities and kingdoms minted their own coins, decorating them with the symbols of the city or the heads of their patron god or kings. Athenian coinage was regarded as being particularly trustworthy and was accepted in many places.

Gold coin minted in the Greek city of Alexandria in Egypt, at the time of Arsinoe III, Queen of Egypt (220–204 BC). It shows the head of Arsinoe and a horn of plenty, symbolizing prosperity.

Coins of the Greek city of Cyrene in North Africa featured the head of the city's patron deity, Zeus Ammon, and the herb silphion. Cyrene was famous for its trade in silphion, which was much used in cooking and medicine of the time.

SUCCESSFUL BUSINESSMEN

A ship of Samos, of which Kolaios was the captain, was carried off course while sailing to Egypt ... and as the wind did not cease to blow until they had passed through the Pillars of Herakles they came to Tartessos, guided by divine providence. Now this trading port was at that time still undiscovered, so that when they returned back home they made a profit from their cargo greater than any other Greeks.

Herodotus

Not every trader was as lucky as Kolaios. Seafaring was dangerous. Cargo might fail to sell or become damaged, and storms might cause shipwrecks. And there was piracy, too. Many pirates roamed the Mediterranean Sea. They were not just lawless adventurers – even honourable aristocrats such as the hero Odysseus raided the coastline on their travels, and piracy was a regular source of income for whole communities.

The Greek trader Sostratos from Aigina was said to have been even wealthier than Kolaios. We know that his voyages took him to Egypt, because he wrote his own name (you can see it scratched into the black zone just below the rim) on a richly painted bowl that he dedicated to the goddess Aphrodite at Naukratis, the Greek trading post in Egypt. Why Aphrodite? She was not just a goddess of love, but she also watched over sea captains.

This pot shows a Greek boat beaching.

Before we young Achaians sailed to Troy, I led men and ships nine times on raids to foreign coasts, and had great luck, taking rich spoils.

Homer (Odysseus is speaking)

GREEKS ABROAD

Greeks established trading posts and settlements all around the Mediterranean. Cities such as Syracuse in Italy, Marseilles in France, Alexandria in Egypt, Odessa in Ukraine and Izmir in Turkey were all originally founded by Greeks. Sometimes the locals fought the Greek settlers, sometimes they welcomed them. In Egypt, the pharaoh gave land to Greek settlers so that they could live and trade in Egypt. They founded the city of Naukratis.

Some Greek craftsmen lived and worked far from home. This fabulous gold brooch was probably made by a Greek goldsmith in Spain.

Many Greeks settled in southern Italy. Here they made pottery that at first looked very similar to the famous Athenian vases, but soon developed its own character – such as this huge and very elaborate deep bowl that was made especially to be placed in a tomb.

The Greeks learned a lot from the foreign peoples they traded and lived with. From the Egyptians they adopted the idea of making life-size statues of young men standing. The Egyptian statue is wearing a kilt, but the Greek statue is naked.

Small, colourful amulets were popular souvenirs from Egypt. This one, in the shape of a little monkey, was brought from Egypt to Cyprus.

FIND OUT MORE

Website on ancient Greece
Explore the world of the ancient Greeks, play games set in ancient Greece, and follow stories of Greek myth and adventure on **www.ancientgreece.co.uk**

Books on ancient Greeks
Peter Connolly and Andrew Solway, *Ancient Greece*, Oxford University Press 2001

Terry Deary and Martin Brown, *The Groovy Greeks (Horrible Histories)*, Scholastic 2007

Andrew Lang, *Tales of Troy and Greece*, Wordsworth Editions 1995

Kate Morton and Ian Jenkins, *Explore the Parthenon: An Ancient Greek Temple*, British Museum Press 2009

Emma McAllister, *Pocket Timeline of Ancient Greece*, British Museum Press 2005

Anne Pearson, *Eyewitness Ancient Greece*, Dorling Kindersley 2002

Sandy Ransford and David Farris, *British Museum Fun Book: Ancient Greece*, British Museum Press 1999

Sean Sheehan, *The British Museum Illustrated Encyclopaedia of Ancient Greece*, British Museum Press 2002; published in the US by Getty Publications 2002

Marcia Williams, *Greek Myths*, Walker Books 2006

Richard Woff, *Pocket Explorer The Ancient Greek World*, British Museum Press 2008

Richard Woff, *Pocket Dictionary Greek & Roman Gods and Goddesses*, British Museum Press 2003; published in the US by Getty Publications 2003

Richard Woff, *Pocket Dictionary Heroes & Heroines of Ancient Greece*, British Museum Press 2004; published in the US by Getty Publications 2004

Books for older readers
Marina Belozerskaya and Kenneth Lapatin, *Ancient Greece: Art, Architecture and History*, Getty Publications 2004

Lucilla Burn, *British Museum Book of Greek and Roman Art*, British Museum Press 2004

John Camp and Elizabeth Fisher, *Exploring the World of the Ancient Greeks*, Thames & Hudson 2002

Peter Connolly and Hazel Dodge, *The Ancient City: Life in Classical Athens and Rome*, Oxford University Press 2000

Robert Garland, *Daily Life of the Ancient Greeks*, Greenwood Press 1998

Charlotte Higgins, *It's All Greek to Me*, Short Books 2008

Jenifer Neils, *The British Museum Concise Introduction Ancient Greece*, British Museum Press 2008

Emma J. Stafford, *Life, Myth and Art in Ancient Greece*, Getty Publications 2004

Alexandra Villing, *A Place in History: Classical Athens*, British Museum Press 2005

Susan Woodford, *An Introduction to Greek Art*, Duckworth 1997

Susan Woodford, *Images of Myths in Classical Antiquity*, Cambridge University Press 2002

INDEX

Achilles 21, 37, 66–7
actors 47, 58–9
aegis cloak 17
Agamemnon 21
agriculture 40–3
Aischylos 50, 58
Alexander the Great 10–11
alphabet 51
Amphitrite 16, 17
amphorae 37, 47, 74–5
animals 23, 26, 28–9, 42–3
Aphrodite 16, 17, 18, 76
Apollo 18, 25, 55, 57
Ares 18
Aristophanes 50, 58
Aristotle 48
armour and weapons 68–9
Artemis 18, 21
artists 34–9
Asklepios 53
Athena 15, 17, 23–4, 36, 42, 74
Athens 4, 10, 12–15, 31, 36–8, 49, 68, 74–5
athletes 5, 31, 60–5

babies 28
Bendis 19
boxing 62, 65
boys 30, 60, 68
burials 33
businessmen 76

chariot racing 63, 65
cheating at sports 65
children 26–33, 44, 46, 60–1, 68
cities 4–5, 9, 14, 61

citizens 12–15
Cleopatra, Queen of Egypt 11
clothes 17, 24, 35, 44, 68–9
coins 5, 11, 74–5
comedies 47, 50, 58–9
cooking 27
craftsmen 17, 34–9, 47, 77

dance 54, 56
death 18, 19, 33
Delphi 18, 25
Demeter 18, 22, 40–1
democracy 5, 12–15, 70
Diogenes 49
Dionysos 18, 58–9
discus-throwing 5, 64
diseases 52
divorce 32
doctors 48, 52–3

education 30–1, 49, 55
entertainers 54–9
Eros 18
Euripides 50, 58–9

families 26–33, 35, 46
farmers 40–3
festivals 23, 41, 55
fish 43
food 23, 40, 42–3, 57
foreigners 15, 35, 45
funerals 33

girls 31–2, 61
gods/goddesses 16–25, 53, 64
gold 39, 75, 77

greaves (shin-guards) 68
growing up 30–1

Hades 19
Hector 21, 66–7
helmets 67, 68
Hephaistos 16, 17, 18, 36
Hera 16–17, 25
Herakles 9, 21
Hermes 18, 57, 75
Herodotus 50
heroes/heroines 8, 9, 13, 20–1, 66–7
Hippokrates 52
Homer 50, 55, 66–7
hoplite soldiers 68
hunters 43

illnesses 52–3
Io 25
Iphigeneia 21

jewellers 39

Kekrops, King 9
kings 8–11
Knossos 8
knucklebones 5, 16, 28

laws 15, 47
lyres 18, 25, 55–7

marriage 17, 32
Mediterranean Sea 5, 72, 74, 77
mercenaries 69
metalworkers 35
Minoans 8

Minos, King of Crete 8, 9
Minotaur 8, 20
money 5, 11, 74–5
music 18, 25, 54–7
Mycenaeans 9

nakedness 35, 62, 77
nurses 28–9, 46

Odysseus 72–3, 76
olives 42
Olympic Games 5, 16, 19, 30, 60–5
oracles 18, 25
ostracism 14

painters 37
palaces 8–9
Pan 16
pankration 62
papyrus 30, 51
Parthenon 14, 24, 38–9, 47
parties (*symposia*) 56–7
Peloponnesian War 50
peplos robe 24
Perikles 14–15
Persephone 18, 19
Persian Empire 11, 13, 69
Persian Wars 50, 70
pets 28–9

phalanx formation 67–8
Pheidias 38
Philip, King of Macedonia 10
philosophers 48–9
Plato 48, 49
playwrights 50, 58–9
poets 50, 54–5, 66–7
Poseidon 16, 17, 20
potters 36–7, 47, 77
priests/priestesses 22–5, 41
Ptolemy I, King of Egypt 11

queens of Egypt 11, 75

religion 22–5, 31

sacrifices 21, 23, 26
sanctuaries 24, 31, 47, 53
Sappho 50
schooling 30–1, 49
sculptors 37, 38–9
sea battles 70–1
servants 31, 44, 46
ships 70, 72
singers 54–5, 57
Sirens 72–3
slaves 26, 27, 28, 44–7
Sokrates 48–9
soldiers 30, 66–71

Sophokles 50, 58
Spartans 30–1, 45, 61, 68
sport 5, 16, 19, 30–1, 60–5
statues 24, 31, 38, 64, 77
symposia (parties) 56–7

temples 22–4, 31, 38–9
theatre 50, 58–9
Theseus 8, 9, 20
thinkers 48–9
toys 28–9
trade 5, 72–7
tragedies 50, 58–9
travel and transport 5, 72–7
Trojan War 21, 50, 66
tyrants 10, 13

Underworld 18, 19, 33

wars 21, 40, 45, 50, 66–71
weddings 32
women 11, 27, 31–2, 35, 61
workshops 34, 47
wrestling 62–3
writers 48, 50–1, 54
writing 51

Zeus 16–17, 19, 65